P9-CQF-553

DATE DUE			

15704

639.3
P

Piers, Helen.

Taking care of your
goldfish

MAERCKER SCHOOL
WESTMONT, IL   60559

686818 01069   13457B   004

MAERCKER DISTRICT 60
SCHOOL LIBRARIES
CLARENDON HILLS, IL 60514

Taking care of your

GOLDFISH

A Young Pet Owner's Guide
by Helen Piers

Consulting Editor: Matthew M. Vriends, Ph.D.

First edition for the United States and Canada
published 1993 by Barron's Educational Series, Inc.
Text copyright © Helen Piers 1993
Illustrations copyright © Helen Piers 1993

First published in Great Britain in 1993 by
Frances Lincoln Limited, Apollo Works
5 Charlton Kings Road, London NW5 2SB

The title of the British edition is *Looking After Your Goldfish*

All rights reserved.
No part of this book may be reproduced in any form,
by photostat, microfilm, xerography, or any other
means, or incorporated into any information retrieval
system, electronic or mechanical, without the written
permission of the copyright owner.

All inquiries should be addressed to:
Barron's Educational Series, Inc.
250 Wireless Boulevard
Hauppauge, NY 11788

Library of Congress Catalog Card No. 92–32170

International Standard Book No. 0-8120-1368-9

Library of Congress Cataloging-in-Publication Data
Piers, Helen.
    Taking care of your goldfish / by Helen Piers : consulting editor,
Matthew M. Vriends.—1st ed.
        p.   cm.—(A young pet owner's guide)
    Includes bibliographical references and index.
    Summary: Includes information on selecting, feeding, and caring
for goldfish as well as instructions on setting up a tank and
breeding and caring for the young.
    ISBN 0-8120-1368-9
    1. Goldfish—Juvenile literature. [1. Goldfish. 2. Pets.]
I. Vriends, Matthew M., 1937–   .   II. Title.   III. Series: Piers,
Helen. Young pet owner's guide.
SF458.G6P55   1993   92-32170
639.3'752—dc20   CIP
                                                        AC

Printed and bound in Hong Kong

3456   987654321

Contents

Keeping goldfish

If you have never kept fish before, goldfish are the best way to start. They are *freshwater* fish so they do not need specially prepared sea water, nor does the water have to be heated as for tropical fish. They are cheap to buy and, after the expense of setting up the aquarium, cost almost nothing to look after.

Many people think that to look after goldfish all you have to do is put them in a glass bowl and give them a pinch of food each day. Actually, keeping goldfish can involve much more than that, and be really interesting.

Keeping goldfish in the old-fashioned type of round bowl is not good for them. It does not give them enough space to swim in, or enough oxygen to breathe, and the curved glass reflects the light in a way that worries them. They are happier and healthier if kept in a fair-sized aquarium tank, and it can be fun arranging this with plants and rocks to look like an underwater pond or stream.

You need to study how to keep the water in the aquarium in the right condition, and find out what food your fish thrive best on. A well cared for goldfish can live for a surprisingly long time — maybe even twenty years. It is also possible to breed goldfish.

This book is mostly about keeping goldfish indoors in an aquarium, but they also can be kept in a garden pond (see page 22).

Goldfish were first bred in China over four thousand years ago from carp-like fish living in ponds and streams. Apart from the *common goldfish* above, many fancy varieties are now bred. Some of these are differently colored from the common goldfish, and some have double tail fins — these are called *fantails*.

Understanding fish

How a fish breathes

Instead of taking in oxygen from the air as we do when we breathe, a fish takes it in from the water by means of its *gills* — folds of fine membrane on either side of its head. It inhales water through its mouth, which then closes, forcing the water to flow over the gills. The oxygen is separated from the water by the gills, and absorbed into the fish's blood. If you watch closely, you can see the *gill covers* opening and closing to let the used water flow out again.

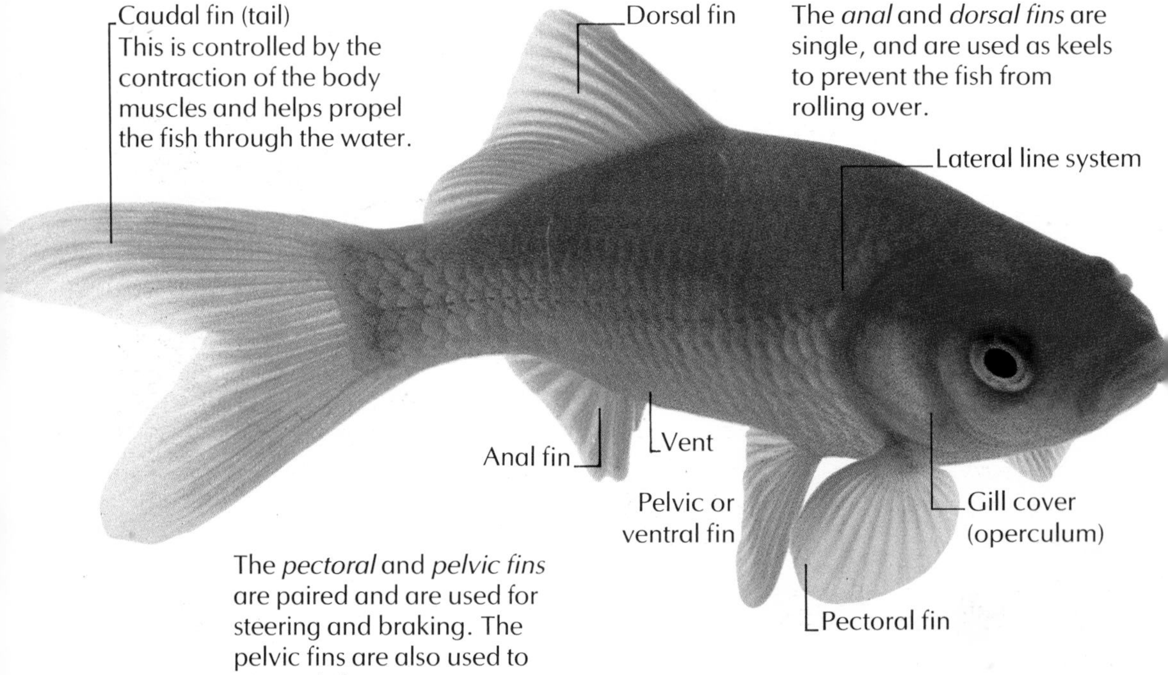

Caudal fin (tail)
This is controlled by the contraction of the body muscles and helps propel the fish through the water.

Dorsal fin

The *anal* and *dorsal fins* are single, and are used as keels to prevent the fish from rolling over.

Lateral line system

Anal fin

Vent

Pelvic or ventral fin

Gill cover (operculum)

The *pectoral* and *pelvic fins* are paired and are used for steering and braking. The pelvic fins are also used to give stability.

Pectoral fin

How a fish swims

A fish uses the muscles of its body to propel itself through the water. It uses its fins for steering, keeping its balance, and braking. Its scales, which are chiefly for protection, also streamline the fish, helping it glide through the water more easily.

How a fish senses

A fish *sees* much as we do, but because its eyes are on either side of its head and protrude slightly, it can see all around without turning.

A fish can *taste* food before taking it into its mouth because it has taste cells both inside and outside the mouth.

Its sense of *touch* is similar to ours.

Its sense of *smell*, though not as strong as in some land-dwelling animals, is still important to a fish for finding its food.

Although a fish can *hear*, it relies more on another sense – a row of pierced scales, called the *lateral line system*, along each side of its body – through which it senses the slightest movement in the water. It uses this sense when hunting live food and escaping from danger.

Fish are *cold-blooded*. This means they have no way of controlling their temperature, and are always as hot or cold as the water around them. A sudden change in the water temperature causes their own temperature to rise or fall just as quickly, and the shock may even prove fatal.

It is interesting to watch a goldfish swimming in the aquarium. You will see that it holds its pectoral fins out in a forward position when it wants to slow down.

Things you will need

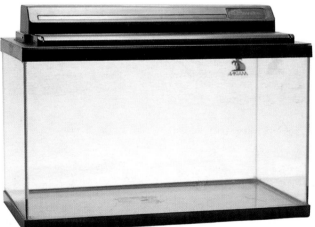

Checklist

- large aquarium and hood
- small plastic tank
- gravel
- rocks
- pebbles
- plants
- aerator and water filter (these are sometimes combined in one unit)
- light unit
- siphon
- glass cleaner (algae scraper)
- net
- thermometer
- food
- feeding ring
- dechlorinator
- biological filter supplement

These pages show you everything you need to keep your fish in the very best condition. When you have read pages 10–13 you will understand better why you need some of this equipment, and how it works.

You will find some expensive equipment on sale, but you should be able to get all you need at a reasonable price.

Goldfish *can* be kept more simply – that is, without an aerator and water filter or an artificial light unit (see pages 11 and 12) – but this does mean giving them more time and care, if they are to be really healthy and long-lived.

Gravel

Rocks

Pebbles

The aquarium tank can be glass as shown, or molded acrylic plastic.

Light unit

Foods and feeding ring
(see page 20)

Net. If you bend the handle
as shown, it makes netting
fish easier.

Scraper for cleaning algae
from the glass

Plants
(See pages
14 and 15.)

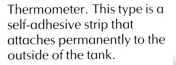

Dechlorinator and
biological filter supplement

Remember

- Make sure the tank you
  buy is big enough for
  the number of fish you
  want to keep (see
  page 13).
- Use number three
  gravel (particle size
  about 3 mm).
- Do not use rocks with
  jagged edges on which
  a fish might hurt itself.
- Do not use soft, soluble
  rocks like limestone and
  sandstone. Granite or
  slate is best.
- *Make sure all electrical
  fittings are well
  insulated.*

Thermometer. This type is a
self-adhesive strip that
attaches permanently to the
outside of the tank.

Siphon for removing water

Small plastic tank with
cover. This is for use as a
"hospital" tank if one of
your fish is ill.

Air pump and water filter
unit. In this setup, the pump
supplies the air needed to
work the filter and at the
same time aerate the water.
Other types of aeration and
filter systems are available
(see page 13).

9

The water

Water is as important to a fish as air is to us. It has to be the right temperature, clean and free from harmful chemicals. It must also hold enough oxygen.

Remember

- Sudden changes in temperature are dangerous for fish.
- Pond or stream water may be polluted.
- Tap water must be treated with a de-chlorinator or stored for two days to allow the chlorine to evaporate.
- A filter unit and biological filter supplement help keep the water clean.
- The water must be well oxygenated.

Temperature

Goldfish thrive best at temperatures between 64.4° and 71.6°F (18° and 22°C), though they *can* live in more extreme temperatures, as long as any change is gradual — not more than two or three degrees a day. *Sudden changes in temperature are very dangerous for fish.*

Which kind of water?

Pond or stream water is *not* good because it may be polluted or contain creatures like dragonfly larvae and water beetles that can harm fish. *Tap water* is best as long as it is properly prepared before being used in the aquarium.

Chlorine, which is added to tap water to make it safe to drink, is poisonous to fish. It can be removed by adding a dechlorinating liquid (sold at pet stores), or by letting the water stand for two days to allow the chlorine to evaporate.

Very hard water should be diluted by mixing it with the same amount of distilled water.

Your pet store will know if the water in your district needs any other special treatment.

In summer, if the water gets too hot (over 75.2°F [24°C]), you can cool it by floating ice cubes in a sealed plastic bag on the surface.

Keeping the water clean

Aquarium water gets polluted unless uneaten food, dead leaves, and the goldfish excreta are removed. A *water filter* helps do this. A liquid *biological filter supplement* (sold at pet stores) should also be added to the water. This boosts the growth of bacteria, which clean the water by breaking down harmful wastes.

Making sure enough oxygen is in the water

As they breathe, fish use up the oxygen in the water and breathe out carbon dioxide – a gas that poisons them if it is not removed and replaced by fresh oxygen. This can only happen where the air outside meets the water – at the surface. Plants help, for they *take in* carbon dioxide, and *add* oxygen to the water. The best way to be sure your fish have enough oxygen is to use an *aerator*. This is an electric pump that pushes air through a porous stone, sending a stream of air bubbles into the tank. The air bubbles themselves are not supplying oxygen, but by keeping the water moving they cause stale water to rise to the surface. There the carbon dioxide can escape and fresh oxygen take its place.

If there is not enough oxygen in the water, the goldfish will swim gasping at the surface in an attempt to take it from the air outside.

Keeping fish without an aerator or filter

This is possible if your house is heated to not more than 68°F (20°C) (cooler water holds more oxygen). You will need to change some of the water each day, grow plants in the aquarium, and add biological filter supplement.

The aquarium tank

You can buy aquarium tanks at most pet stores and aquarium suppliers.

Tanks can be made of glass or molded plastic. Glass is heavier than plastic, but plastic gets scratched more easily.

Remember, the more water surface a tank provides, the more oxygen will be in the water. So a wide, shallower tank is better than a narrow, deeper one that holds the same amount of water. And the more fish, the more oxygen they will need, so the bigger the tank must be.

The best place to keep the tank

Choose a room where the temperature does not vary a lot between day and nighttime, and avoid placing the tank near a fire or radiator.

Fish and plants both need light. This can be supplied by a light unit fixed to the tank hood, or by natural daylight. It is possible to keep goldfish without artificial light, if the tank gets plenty of daylight. But make sure that no direct sun shines onto the tank, making it too hot. You will know the tank is not getting enough light if the plants grow tall and straggly. If it is getting too much, algae will appear on the glass and turn the water green.

You can buy stands for larger aquariums. Smaller ones can be kept on a table or shelf provided it is level and strong enough to carry the weight.

The hood (or lid) stops things from falling into the tank, the goldfish from jumping out, and – most important – it keeps them safe from cats!

The light unit is fixed inside the hood. A fluorescent strip is better than light bulbs, which tend to give off too much heat. The tank will need ten hours a day under a 20-watt strip.

You can work out how many fish can be kept in your tank by using this simple rule: **for every ¼-inch (6 mm) of fish's length (including tail) allow about 1 quart (1 L) of water.** So a 40-quart (40 L) tank would be big enough for four 2½-inch (6 cm) fish.

But do not forget that your fish will grow.

Remember

- Make sure the tank is on a firm, level base. A piece of expanded polystyrene cut to size and placed underneath helps cushion any unevenness.
- *Never* keep the tank by a radiator, a fire, or a window that gets direct sun. It will get too hot.
- Leave enough space above the tank so you can reach in to clean it.
- Electrical fittings must be well insulated against contact with water.
- Sudden changes in light shock fish. So, switch the tank light off ten minutes before the other lights in the room.

◢ This **aerator and water filter** is an underwater unit combining an electric pump and water filter in one. The two can be separate (see pages 9 and 17). There are also "undergravel" filters — plastic plates laid on the bottom of the tank under the gravel. These are a little more complicated to use.

Whichever type you buy, follow the manufacturer's instructions carefully.

The plants

You will need plants for your aquarium. Apart from making it look attractive, plants provide shade and hiding places for the goldfish, and add oxygen to the water.

Where to obtain water plants

Suitable floating plants are Duckweed (above) and Fairy Moss. Floating plants grow very fast, so you may have to thin them out if they begin to cover the surface and cut out too much light.

It is safest to buy plants from an aquarium supplier or pet store. If you gather plants from ponds and streams there is the danger they may carry disease and harbor the eggs of creatures that, when they hatch, will harm the fish.

Some rooting plants for the aquarium:

Hairgrass (*Eleocharis*)   *Fittonia*   Fanwort *(Cabomba)*   Dwarf Rush *(Acorus)*

Which types of plants

Some types of water plants put down roots in the gravel at the bottom, and others float on the surface.

Of the rooting plants, some will grow tall and look best at the back and sides of the tank. The more bushy kinds are useful for filling spaces in the center, and others, which will only grow short and tufty, should be planted in the front. When you buy your plants be sure to ask which type they are, so you will know where they will look best in the aquarium.

To disinfect new plants, you can soak them for half an hour in water with a few grains of potassium permanganate added. The solution must be weak – pink, *not* purple. Rinse the plants well afterwards.

Eel-grass (*Vallisneria*) Water Milfoil Canadian Pondweed Arrowhead (*Sagittaria*)
(*Myriophyllum*) (*Elodia*)

Setting up the aquarium

Remember

- Carry the empty tank with your hands under it – carrying by the sides causes leaks.
- *Never* use detergent, soap or disinfectant.
- **Get an electrician or other grown-up to check that electrical fittings are well insulated and plugs wired up correctly. *Never* put your hands in the water when the electricity is on.**

You need to set up the aquarium at least a week before you put any fish into it. This gives it time to settle down and allows the plants to begin to take root.

First you will need to wash out the tank with a tablespoon of salt in the water. *Do not use detergent, soap, or disinfectant* – all are poisonous to fish. Now is the time to test the tank for leaks. These can be repaired with aquarium sealant.

Then the tank should be positioned where it is to stay permanently. When full of water it will be heavy, and moving it could cause leaks.

Once the tank is clean and in place, you can begin to set it up. Follow these simple steps. Work carefully, and take plenty of time to think about where everything should go.

1. Wash half a bucketful of gravel at a time under running water, until the water is clear.

Cover the bottom of the tank with damp gravel – 2½ inches (6 cm) deep in back, sloping to 1¼ inches (3 cm) in front.

2. Fix the water filter box towards the back of the tank, and connect it to the pump by means of the plastic tubing. Do **not** switch on the pump. Now arrange the rocks as you think they look best.

3. Partly fill the tank with water. If you place a shallow bowl in the tank and direct a *gentle* flow of water into it, this will stop the gravel from being disturbed.

   Now you can put in the rooting plants.

4. Use a finger to spread the roots of each plant under the gravel. Then pull the plant up gently until the place where the stem meets the root is just above the gravel. Place pebbles around it to anchor it, or use plant anchors (sold at pet stores).

5. When you finish planting, fill the tank with water (to about 1 inch [2 cm] from the top). Add dechlorinator **first** and then biological supplement. Before you put in the floating plants, remove scum by drawing clean paper across the surface.

6. Place the hood on top. Plug in the lighting unit and air pump – **be sure no electric wires are touching the water**. Let the aquarium stand for a week or more, with the right amount of light and aerator and filter working, before you add fish.

Buying goldfish

You can buy goldfish at pet stores, aquarium suppliers and some garden centers. You will find them advertised in fishkeeping magazines, and some fishkeeping societies hold shows where they are offered for sale.

Which kind of goldfish?

It is best to begin by keeping the common goldfish, and move on to the more exotic varieties (see page 29) when you have had some experience of fishkeeping, because these are less hardy and need special care.

When you go to buy your goldfish you will find they are kept in open tanks as shown, or in aquariums. You will be able to watch them swimming about, and take your time choosing the ones you want.

Your fish will be given to you in a plastic bag of water at the temperature they are used to.

Fish cannot survive sudden changes in temperature. So, if the weather is really cold, cover your goldfish with a scarf or newspaper during the journey home.

How many fish?

This depends on the size of your tank. But, in any case, if you are setting up a new aquarium, you should start with only one or two fish.

The filtration system in a new aquarium cannot cope with too many fish at the beginning.

If your tank is big enough, you can add more fish in a few weeks' time.

Which sex are they?

You can only tell the sex of a fish when it is in breeding condition (see page 26). But if you wish to breed goldfish and you eventually have four or five fish, with luck you will have at least one of each sex.

How to choose healthy fish

A healthy fish should have a gently rounded body. The eyes should be bright, the scales clean, without wounds or spots, and the fins not frayed or damaged.

A healthy fish swims actively with its dorsal fin erect. Never buy a fish that is swimming on its side or with its fins clamped shut.

It is not a good idea to buy fish from a tank in which the water is cloudy or there are dead or sick fish.

Taking your fish home

Your fish will be given to you in a plastic bag of water at the temperature they are used to. This will hold enough oxygen to last until you get home.

When you get home, float the unopened bag in the aquarium for half an hour. By this time the water in the bag will be about the same temperature as that in the aquarium, and you can safely open the bag and let the fish swim out.

Feeding

Goldfish should be fed on packaged dried food, as well as some live food.

Packaged dried food

Make sure this is labeled *"goldfish"* food, not just "fish" or "aquarium" food. Goldfish need different food from other fish.

Live food

Dried food makes a good basic diet, but your fish also need some live food. Most pet stores stock live water fleas (*Daphnia*) and freshwater shrimp. *Tubifex* worms also can be given, but these often carry disease. For the same reason it is better not to catch food for your fish in ponds. When live food is not available you can buy the same foods freeze-dried.

Some goldfish also enjoy occasional scraps of lettuce or spinach, peas, and scrapings of raw *lean* meat. Take care to remove these if not eaten at once. Scraps of meat can be dangled in the water on pieces of thread so they are easy to lift out if not eaten.

How much and how often?

Feed dried food twice a day at the same time each day. *Never* overfeed. Give only as much as the fish eat in *five to ten minutes*. Any food left uneaten must be removed with a net.

Feed live food once a week. You need not be afraid of giving too much live food, because it will not pollute the water if not eaten at once.

Remember

- *Never* overfeed.
- *Never* give fatty foods.
- Remove uneaten food at once, or it will pollute the water.
- Give as much variety of food as possible.
- Feed at the same times each day.

To find out how much food your fish are going to need, float a few flakes on the surface. As this is eaten, add more little by little. Remember, the fish will have taken all they need in five to ten minutes.

Using a feeding ring keeps the water cleaner.

Looking after the aquarium

Once a day

Check fish for illness. Check temperature. Make sure the aerator is working. *If not using an aerator or filter,* siphon off a cupful of water and replace with fresh water.*

Once a week

Siphon off 10 percent of the water, and replace with fresh water.* Remove dead leaves and thin out plants as needed. Remove algae from glass using an algae scraper (see page 9).

Once a month

Take out the filter medium – foam or floss material inside the filter box. Rinse in water and replace. (Some filters have a disposable medium that has to be renewed instead of rinsed.) Add biological filter supplement, following instructions on the bottle. *If not using a filter* just add the supplement.

*Any water added must be at the same temperature as that in the aquarium. It must be dechlorinated (see page 10).

To siphon off water, place a bucket with a little water already in it below the level of the tank. Put the nozzle end of the siphon tube in the tank, and the other end under the water in the bucket. Now squeeze the bulb and the water will be drawn up out of the tank and down into the bucket. Always siphon off water from the bottom, where it gets dirtiest.

The goldfish pond

Remember

- *Never* let the pond get clogged with dead plants or falling leaves.
- *Never* use chemicals to clear the water of unwanted algae.
- To protect fish from cats and birds, and prevent leaves from falling in, you can cover the pond with fine mesh netting.
- Use a pond-heater or float balls on the surface to stop the pond from freezing over.
- *Never* try to break the ice with a hammer.

You will need plants in your pond to provide the fish with shelter and food. Floating plants like water lilies (above) give the best shade for the fish.

Goldfish kept in a pond are of course in danger from predators, but they do have the advantages of live food to eat and more space to swim around than in an aquarium.

To be suitable for goldfish the pond should be at least 2½ feet (80 cm) deep, with a shallow area at one end where they can *spawn* (lay their eggs). In a shallower pond changes in temperature would be too rapid, and there would be the danger of it overheating in summer and freezing solid during winter.

You need to allow roughly 11 square feet (1 m^2) of pond for five average 4½ to 6½ inch (10–15 cm) fish.

Aeration

Pond water is moved about naturally by wind and rain, so it usually holds enough oxygen. In very hot, still weather if you see the fish gasping at the surface you can play the garden hose on the pond for a few minutes to aerate it. Aerator pumps are also available for use in ponds.

Feeding

Your goldfish will find enough live food in the pond, but they still need feeding with packaged dried food during most of the year. Feed once a day and give only as much as is eaten in ten minutes. They will take extra in late summer, ready for the winter when they go into semihibernation at the bottom and do not eat. Never put food in the pond during winter.

The winter

Goldfish spend the winter burrowed into the mud at the bottom of the pond where it is warmer. There is a danger that if the pond freezes over they could die through lack of oxygen. To prevent this you can use a floating pond heater (installed by an electrician), or you can simply float a large ball or two on the surface so that if the water freezes, holes are left through which air can pass.

If removing ice, do this at the edge where it is thinner. *Never* break the ice with a hammer. The vibrations will shock and harm the fish.

Pond maintenance

If you regularly clear the pond of dead and overgrown plants, it will only need emptying and cleaning thoroughly once in three years. This is best done in autumn or spring.

Blanketweed – a fast-growing algae – must be removed regularly using a stick, so that it does not choke other plants.

It is also important to clear out dead plants and falling leaves, especially in the autumn. If left to rot during the winter, they will pollute the water and harm the fish.

In spring, when the fish begin to appear near the surface, watch them for signs of illness – they may be weak after the winter. Remove any sick ones, and give them a salt bath (see page 25) at the same temperature as the pond water.

Illnesses

If one of your fish is ill, you should move it to the hospital tank. Always use a net and be careful not to damage its delicate fins.

Goldfish are more likely to get ill if they are in a run–down, weak condition. This can be caused by too little variety of food, polluted water, lack of oxygen, or by shock from a sudden change in temperature or light, or from strong vibrations, like knocking on the aquarium glass.

But disease attacks even the best cared for fish, so it is important to inspect your fish daily and, if one of them shows signs of illness, move it to the hospital tank where you can give it treatment and prevent it passing on infection to the others. The water must be the same temperature as in the aquarium, and be dechlorinated. A few plastic plants will give the sick fish shelter.

Quarantine

Any new fish should be kept in the hospital tank for one week before they are put in the aquarium, to make sure they are not carrying disease.

Watch for any fish that is not eating well, holds its fins close to its body, and spends most of the time resting at the bottom. It is probably not well. If you do not know what is wrong with it, you can try adding a general tonic (sold at pet stores), to the water. Do not worry if this changes the water green.

These are some of the more common illnesses a goldfish can suffer from, with some suggestions about what to do. But do not put off getting advice from your pet store or aquarium supplier if one of your fish is ill.

Symptoms	Possible cause and what to do
The fish is covered with white spots, like grains of sugar	This may be *White Spot (Ich)* and is caused by parasites. The pet store will give you medication to put in the water. *This is not the same as the white spots seen on the gill covers of male fish during the breeding season.*
The fish is covered with what look like tiny cotton balls	It has *fungus* disease, so it must be isolated to avoid infecting the other fish. You can buy medication to treat this disease. A mildly affected fish can be cured by giving it a salt bath daily. To prepare this, add one heaping teaspoon of **sea** or **aquarium salt** for each quart of dechlorinated or aquarium water, and keep the fish in it for 15 minutes. Dilute if the fish seems distressed. Live food will help recovery.
The fins look frayed as the tissue wastes away	This is *fin rot* and is usually caused by bad aquarium conditions, or poor food. Use medication or salt treatment (as above).
The fish has feces trailing from its vent	This is a sign of *constipation*. It can be cured by giving more greens and live food.
The fish spends its time gasping at the surface	This is a sign of oxygen starvation. The water must be aerated at once, either with an aerator, or by a partial water change and gentle agitation. In the case of a pond, a hose played on the surface will help.

Breeding

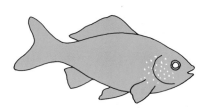

The first thing you notice when the fish are ready to spawn is that a *male* (above) has white spots on his gill covers, which may extend up to the foremost part of the pectoral fins.

A *female* will appear swollen, because she is carrying eggs.

Goldfish eggs look like tiny pinheads in jelly and stick to the plants – each one separately.

Although goldfish are probably the easiest fish to breed, it can be disappointing when, as can happen, very few of the young survive. You have to be patient and remember that although fish lay hundreds of eggs at one spawning (mating), it is natural for a large number to fail to reach adulthood. In the wild, many become food for other animals, and many more do not survive either through disease or lack of food.

Preparing the fish for breeding

Goldfish breed during spring and summer, and each fish can spawn once a month. In early spring you should begin to feed up your goldfish, giving them plenty of protein, like Daphnia, freshwater shrimps, and shredded raw meat. Also make sure the water is clean and well-oxygenated, or they will not spawn.

Breeding goldfish in an aquarium

Breeding in an aquarium is more successful if any pair of fish in breeding condition are moved into a separate tank, which later becomes the hatching tank for the young. This is prepared in the same way as the aquarium, but without rocks. It is then divided by a well-fitting glass partition. The fish are kept one on either side of the glass for a few days, after which it is taken away to allow them to spawn. Spawning can begin in the morning and go on all day. Afterwards the two fish are put back into the aquarium, and the eggs left to hatch.

How fish behave when spawning

You will know the fish are spawning when the male begins to chase the female about, making a lot of splashing and upheaval. This causes her to release her eggs, which he then covers with *milt* (sperm) to fertilize them.

Breeding goldfish in a pond

In a pond, breeding will take place naturally, as long as the fish are fed well in early spring. The eggs are best brought in still attached to their plants and placed in a tank as above. This way they will not be eaten by water snails, insect larvae, and even adult goldfish.

The eggs will hatch in about three to four days. Ideally the water temperature should be 70° to 75°F (21°–25°C).

Ideally, the tank in which you put your goldfish for breeding should be as much as 3 feet (90 cm) long, and the water relatively shallow. There should be gravel at the bottom, and a dense clump of fine-leaved plants at one end, but no rocks on which the fish could hurt themselves while chasing around the tank.

The young

The new fish will hang like hairs from the plants for a few days before they become free-swimming. *At this stage, be careful to keep the surface of the water free from scum by dragging a piece of clean paper across it.* This is because the *fry* (young fish) need to gulp in air from outside to fill their swim bladders. (The swim bladder is what keeps a fish afloat.)

It is also essential to feed them as soon as they are free-swimming. You can buy liquid food specially prepared for fry.

At *one month* you can give adult food.

At *three months* the young fish can join the adult fish in the aquarium or pond.

You may have been very successful and bred more young than you want to keep. If you do not have friends who would like them for their pond or aquarium, your local pet store may be glad to buy them from you.

The young fish (fry) are a dull olive green. They will not have the bright red-golden color of an adult goldfish until they are a year old.

Fancy varieties

If you have enjoyed keeping your goldfish, sooner or later you will probably want to add some of the more exotic varieties to your aquarium or pond.

Although all of the many varieties of goldfish were originally bred from the common goldfish, many look very different. Some are different in color and body shape or have protruding telescopic eyes, and others may have long flowing fins. Many have double caudal and anal fins. These are called *fantails*.

On the whole, these fancy goldfish need careful handling, for they are delicate. They are not as hardy as the common goldfish and, if kept in a pond, should be brought indoors in winter.

The *Fantail* (above) is a graceful twin-tail with a rounded, rather egg-shaped body and flowing fins.

The *Comet* (on the right) has a slim body that helps it move fast through the water. Its deeply-forked tail can be almost as long again as its body; the other fins also tend to taper to a point.

The *Shubunkin* is another beautiful streamlined fish with unusual coloring and an enormous tail. It is an active fish, requiring a large tank.

Whether you keep your goldfish in an aquarium or a pond, you soon will get to know one from the other by the way they behave. Some come more readily for their food and others are more active swimmers.

You also can have fun training your goldfish to come for their food when you whistle. When they are really tame, some goldfish even will leap out of the water to take the food from your fingers.

Useful information

Eggs hatch in	4–14 days
Fry need feeding when free-swimming	3 days later
Adult food given at	1 month
Fry can join adults at	3 months
Fish reach full color at	1 year
Best age to breed	2½–3 years
Spawning season	April–September
Length at 5 years (common goldfish)	8 inches (20 cm)
Maximum length (common goldfish)	16 inches (40 cm)
Outgrow aquarium and must be moved to pond when	6 inches (15 cm)
Life expectancy common goldfish	20 years
fancy goldfish	12 years

Further Reading

Goldfish
Marshall Ostrow
A Complete Pet Owner's Manual
Barron's, Hauppauge, New York, 1985

Goldfish and Ornamental Carp
B. Penzes and I. Tölg
Barron's, Hauppauge, New York, 1986

Water Plants in the Aquarium
Ines Scheurmann
Barron's, Hauppauge, New York, 1987

MAERCKER DISTRICT 60
SCHOOL LIBRARIES
CLARENDON HILLS, IL 60514

Index